Defeating Bipolar Disorder

A Simple Guide For You And Your Loved Ones

Gianna Evelyn

Table of Contents

Chapter 1 ---5

What You Need To Know --5

When is a Mood Considered Abnormal? --------------------------------------5

Understanding Mania--8

Stages of Mania---10

Chapter 2 --14

Diagnosis of Bipolar Disorder--14

DSM--14

Diagnostic Process---18

Chapter 3 --23

Types of Bipolar Disorders --23

Bipolar I Disorder ---23

Bipolar II Disorder --25

Cyclothymic Disorder ---27

Soft Bipolar Disorder--28

Schizoaffective Disorder ---30

Other Specified Bipolar and Related Disorders -----------------------32

Chapter 4 --36

Causes Of Bipolar Disorders --36

The Brain's Role --36

How the Body Handles Stress--40

The Role Hormones Play --42

Chronobiology ---45

Circadian Rhythms And Bipolar Disorder -----------------------45

Understanding Circadian Rhythms ---------------------------------46

Circadian Rhythms and Bipolar Disorder ----------------------46

The Role of Clock Genes ------------------------------------47

Impact on Mood Episodes -----------------------------------47

Genetics And Bipolar Disorder ----------------------------------48

Chapter 5 --51

Treatments --51

Meditation---51

Mood Stabilizing Medications----------------------------------54

Antidepressant Medications-----------------------------------58

Pipeline Drugs For Bipolar Disorders--------------------------63

Importance Of A Diet --67

Alcohol And Drug Abuse-----------------------------------70

Brain Stimulation Treatments---------------------------------73

Importance Of Psychotherapy---------------------------------78

Chapter 6 ---83

Beginning To Thrive---83

Confronting And Accepting The Illness ------------------------83

Importance of Mood Hygiene --------------------------------87

Supporting Someone With Bipolar Disorder -------------------90

Legal Issues---94

Chapter 7 ---98

Conclusion--98

Resources --102

Support Organizations---------------------------------------102

Additional Reading ---103

Chapter 1

What You Need To Know

When is a Mood Considered Abnormal?

A mood can be described as abnormal when it deviates significantly from typical emotional responses and affects an individual's ability to function in daily life. Here are key indicators that a mood may be considered abnormal:

1. Intensity and Duration

- **Overly Intense**: The mood is much stronger than what would be expected in a given situation. For example, feeling extremely elated or excessively sad without a clear reason.
- **Persistent**: The mood lasts for an extended period, often weeks or months, rather than fluctuating with circumstances.

2. Impact on Daily Functioning

- **Impaired Functioning**: The mood interferes with the person's ability to perform daily activities, such as work, school, or social interactions. This can include difficulty concentrating, making decisions, or maintaining relationships.
- **Behavioral Changes**: Significant changes in behavior, such as withdrawing from social activities, neglecting personal hygiene, or engaging in risky behaviors.

3. Accompanied by Other Symptoms

- **Sleep Disturbances**: Changes in sleep patterns, such as insomnia or excessive sleeping.
- **Appetite Changes**: Noticeable changes in appetite or weight, either an increase or decrease.
- **Energy Levels**: Unusual levels of energy, either feeling excessively energetic (mania) or extremely fatigued (depression).
- **Cognitive Impairments**: Difficulty with thinking, memory, or decision-making.

4. Emotional Extremes

- **Depression**: Persistent feelings of sadness, hopelessness, or worthlessness. This can include a lack of interest in activities once enjoyed and thoughts of self-harm or suicide.

- **Mania**: Periods of abnormally elevated mood, increased activity, and energy levels. This can include impulsive behavior, rapid speech, and grandiose ideas.
- **Mixed Episodes**: Experiencing symptoms of both mania and depression simultaneously, which can be particularly distressing and confusing.

5. Context and Appropriateness

- **Inappropriate Reactions**: Emotional responses that are disproportionate to the situation. For example, laughing uncontrollably at a sad event or feeling intense anger over a minor inconvenience.
- **Lack of Trigger**: Experiencing intense emotions without any identifiable cause or trigger.

6. Duration and Frequency

- **Chronicity**: The mood persists for a long time, often beyond what is typical for a given situation.
- **Recurrent Episodes**: Frequent episodes of abnormal mood, such as repeated bouts of depression or mania.

Understanding Mania

Mania is a state of abnormally elevated mood, arousal, and energy levels. It is a hallmark symptom of bipolar disorder, particularly Bipolar I Disorder. Mania can significantly impact a person's ability to function and may require medical intervention.

Key Characteristics of Mania

1. **Elevated Mood**:
    Euphoria: An intense feeling of happiness and well-being, often without a clear reason.
    Irritability: Increased irritability and agitation, especially when others do not share the individual's high energy or ideas.
2. **Increased Energy and Activity**:
    Hyperactivity: Engaging in multiple activities simultaneously, often without completing them.
    Restlessness: Inability to sit still or relax, constantly needing to move or do something.
3. **Reduced Need for Sleep**:
    Insomnia: Sleeping very little without feeling tired. Some individuals may go days with minimal sleep.
4. **Racing Thoughts and Rapid Speech**:

- **Flight of Ideas**: Rapidly jumping from one idea to another, making it difficult for others to follow the conversation.
- **Pressured Speech**: Talking quickly and incessantly, often loudly and with a sense of urgency.

5. **Impulsivity and Poor Judgment**:
   - **Risky Behaviors**: Engaging in activities with high potential for negative consequences, such as excessive spending, reckless driving, or unprotected sex.
   - **Grandiosity**: Inflated self-esteem or unrealistic beliefs in one's abilities and powers.

6. **Distractibility**:
   - **Easily Distracted**: Difficulty maintaining focus on one task, easily diverted by external stimuli.

7. **Psychotic Symptoms** (in severe cases):
   - **Delusions**: Strongly held false beliefs, such as thinking one has special powers or is on a special mission.
   - **Hallucinations**: Seeing or hearing things that are not present.

Mania, a key feature of bipolar disorder, can be categorized into different stages based on the severity and impact of symptoms. Understanding these stages can help in recognizing the progression of manic episodes and seeking appropriate treatment.

1. Hypomania

Hypomania is the mildest form of mania. It is characterized by elevated mood and increased activity levels, but the symptoms are not severe enough to cause significant impairment in social or occupational functioning. People experiencing hypomania may feel more productive and creative, but their behavior is noticeably different from their usual self.

Key Symptoms:

- Elevated mood: Feeling unusually happy or euphoric.
- Increased energy: More active and energetic than usual.
- Reduced need for sleep: Feeling rested after only a few hours of sleep.
- Increased talkativeness: Speaking more rapidly and frequently.
- Racing thoughts: Jumping from one idea to another quickly.

Distractibility: Easily distracted by external stimuli.

Engaging in risky behaviors: Mildly impulsive actions, such as spending sprees or taking on new projects.

2. Acute Mania

Acute mania is more severe than hypomania and can cause significant impairment in daily functioning. During an acute manic episode, individuals may exhibit extreme behaviors and require medical intervention to prevent harm to themselves or others.

Key Symptoms:

Extreme euphoria or irritability: Intense feelings of happiness or anger.

Grandiosity: Inflated self-esteem and unrealistic beliefs in one's abilities.

Decreased need for sleep: Little to no sleep without feeling tired.

Pressured speech: Talking very fast, often with a sense of urgency.

Flight of ideas: Rapidly shifting from one topic to another, making it hard for others to follow.

Increased goal-directed activity: Engaging in multiple activities simultaneously, often without completing them.

- Risky behaviors: Engaging in dangerous activities, such as reckless driving, unprotected sex, or excessive spending.
- Psychotic symptoms: In severe cases, individuals may experience delusions (false beliefs) or hallucinations (seeing or hearing things that are not there).

3. Delirious Mania

Delirious mania (also known as **manic delirium**) is the most severe form of mania. It is characterized by extreme agitation, confusion, and psychosis. This stage is a medical emergency and requires immediate hospitalization.

Key Symptoms:

- Severe agitation: Intense restlessness and inability to stay still.
- Confusion: Disorientation and difficulty understanding what is happening around them.
- Psychosis: Severe delusions and hallucinations, often leading to dangerous behaviors.
- Catatonia: In some cases, individuals may become unresponsive or exhibit bizarre postures.

- Extreme risk-taking: Engaging in highly dangerous activities without regard for consequences.

Chapter 2

Diagnosis of Bipolar Disorder

DSM

The **Diagnostic and Statistical Manual of Mental Disorders, Fifth Edition (DSM-5)**, is a comprehensive classification system used by mental health professionals to diagnose and classify mental disorders. Published by the American Psychiatric Association (APA), the DSM-5 provides standardized criteria for the diagnosis of mental health conditions.

Purpose of the DSM-5

The DSM-5 serves several key purposes:

- Standardization: It provides a common language and standard criteria for the classification of mental disorders, ensuring consistency in diagnosis across different healthcare settings.
- Clinical Utility: It aids clinicians in diagnosing and treating mental health conditions by offering clear definitions and criteria.

- Research: It supports research by providing a standardized framework for studying mental health conditions.

Structure of the DSM-5

The DSM-5 is organized into three main sections:

- Section I: Introduction and use of the manual, including instructions on how to use the diagnostic criteria.
- Section II: Diagnostic criteria and codes for all recognized mental disorders, organized into chapters based on related conditions.
- Section III: Emerging measures and models, including assessment tools, cultural formulations, and conditions that require further research.

Diagnostic Criteria

For each disorder, the DSM-5 provides a set of diagnostic criteria that must be met for a diagnosis to be made. These criteria typically include:

- Symptom Requirements: Specific symptoms that must be present, along with the duration and severity of these symptoms.
- Exclusion Criteria: Conditions or symptoms that must be ruled out to avoid misdiagnosis.

- Functional Impairment: Evidence that the symptoms cause significant distress or impairment in social, occupational, or other important areas of functioning.

Major Diagnostic Categories

The DSM-5 includes a wide range of mental health conditions, categorized into several major groups, such as:

- Neurodevelopmental Disorders: Includes ADHD, autism spectrum disorder, and intellectual disabilities.
- Schizophrenia Spectrum and Other Psychotic Disorders: Includes schizophrenia, schizoaffective disorder, and delusional disorder.
- Bipolar and Related Disorders: Includes bipolar I disorder, bipolar II disorder, and cyclothymic disorder.
- Depressive Disorders: Includes major depressive disorder, persistent depressive disorder (dysthymia), and disruptive mood dysregulation disorder.
- Anxiety Disorders: Includes generalized anxiety disorder, panic disorder, and social anxiety disorder.

- Obsessive-Compulsive and Related Disorders: Includes obsessive-compulsive disorder (OCD), body dysmorphic disorder, and hoarding disorder.
- Trauma- and Stressor-Related Disorders: Includes posttraumatic stress disorder (PTSD) and acute stress disorder.
- Feeding and Eating Disorders: Includes anorexia nervosa, bulimia nervosa, and binge-eating disorder.

Cultural Considerations

The DSM-5 emphasizes the importance of cultural context in diagnosing mental disorders. It includes a Cultural Formulation Interview (CFI) to help clinicians understand the cultural background of patients and how it may influence their symptoms and experiences.

Changes from DSM-IV to DSM-5

The transition from DSM-IV to DSM-5 included several significant changes:

- Removal of the Multiaxial System: The DSM-5 eliminated the multiaxial system used in DSM-IV, which categorized diagnoses into five axes. Instead, it integrates all relevant information into a single diagnostic framework.

- New Disorders: The DSM-5 introduced new disorders, such as disruptive mood dysregulation disorder and hoarding disorder.
- Revised Criteria: Diagnostic criteria for several disorders were revised to reflect new research findings and clinical experience.

Use in Clinical Practice

The DSM-5 is widely used by mental health professionals, including psychiatrists, psychologists, social workers, and counselors. It guides the diagnostic process, informs treatment planning, and facilitates communication among healthcare providers.

Diagnostic Process

Diagnosing bipolar disorder involves a comprehensive evaluation process to accurately identify the condition and differentiate it from other mental health disorders.
1. Initial Assessment

The diagnostic process typically begins with an initial assessment by a healthcare provider, which includes:

- **Medical History**: Gathering detailed information about the patient's medical history, including any previous mental health issues, family history of mood disorders, and any medications or substances being used.
- **Symptom Review**: Discussing the patient's symptoms, including their duration, frequency, and severity. This helps in identifying patterns that may indicate bipolar disorder.

2. Physical Examination

A physical exam is conducted to rule out any medical conditions that could be causing the symptoms. This may include:

- **Vital Signs**: Checking blood pressure, heart rate, and other vital signs.
- **Laboratory Tests**: Blood tests and other laboratory tests to rule out conditions such as thyroid disorders, which can mimic symptoms of bipolar disorder.

3. Psychiatric Evaluation

A thorough psychiatric evaluation is crucial for diagnosing bipolar disorder. This involves:

- **Clinical Interviews**: Conducting detailed interviews with the patient to understand their thoughts, feelings, and behavior patterns. Input from family members or close friends can also be valuable.

- **Psychological Assessments**: Using standardized questionnaires and rating scales to assess mood, behavior, and cognitive function. Common tools include the Mood Disorder Questionnaire (MDQ) and the Young Mania Rating Scale (YMRS).

4. Mood Charting

Patients may be asked to keep a mood diary or chart to track their mood changes over time. This helps in identifying patterns and triggers for mood episodes.

5. Diagnostic Criteria

The diagnosis of bipolar disorder is based on criteria outlined in the **Diagnostic and Statistical Manual of Mental Disorders (DSM-5)**. The DSM-5 criteria for bipolar disorder include:

- **Bipolar I Disorder**: Characterized by at least one manic episode lasting at least one week, which may be preceded or followed by hypomanic or depressive episodes.
- **Bipolar II Disorder**: Involves at least one hypomanic episode and one major depressive episode, without a full manic episode.

- **Cyclothymic Disorder**: Characterized by periods of hypomanic symptoms and periods of depressive symptoms lasting for at least two years, but not meeting the full criteria for hypomanic or depressive episodes.

6. Differential Diagnosis

It is essential to differentiate bipolar disorder from other mental health conditions that may present with similar symptoms, such as:

- **Major Depressive Disorder**: Characterized by depressive episodes without manic or hypomanic episodes.
- **Attention-Deficit/Hyperactivity Disorder (ADHD)**: Symptoms of impulsivity and hyperactivity can overlap with manic episodes.
- **Borderline Personality Disorder (BPD)**: Both conditions can involve mood instability, but BPD is characterized by a pervasive pattern of instability in interpersonal relationships, self-image, and emotions.

7. Collaborative Approach

Diagnosing bipolar disorder often involves a collaborative approach, including input from:

- **Psychiatrists**: Specialists in mental health who can provide a comprehensive evaluation and diagnosis.
- **Psychologists**: Professionals who can conduct psychological assessments and provide therapy.
- **Primary Care Physicians**: Doctors who can rule out medical conditions and coordinate care.

Chapter 3

Types of Bipolar Disorders

Bipolar I Disorder

Bipolar I Disorder is a severe mental health condition characterized by extreme mood swings, including manic episodes and often depressive episodes.

Key Features

- **Manic Episodes:** The hallmark of Bipolar I Disorder is the presence of at least one manic episode. A manic episode is a period of abnormally elevated, expansive, or irritable mood and increased activity or energy lasting at least one week, or any duration if hospitalization is necessary.
- **Depressive Episodes:** While not required for diagnosis, most individuals with Bipolar I Disorder also experience major depressive episodes, characterized by persistent feelings of sadness, hopelessness, and loss of interest in activities.

Symptoms

Manic Episode Symptoms:

- **Elevated Mood:** Feeling overly happy, energetic, or irritable.
- **Increased Activity:** Engaging in multiple activities simultaneously, often with little need for sleep.
- **Grandiosity:** Inflated self-esteem or unrealistic beliefs in one's abilities.
- **Rapid Speech:** Talking quickly, often jumping from one topic to another.
- **Impulsivity:** Engaging in risky behaviors, such as spending sprees, reckless driving, or unprotected sex.

Depressive Episode Symptoms:

- **Persistent Sadness:** Feeling down or hopeless for most of the day.
- **Loss of Interest:** No longer finding pleasure in activities once enjoyed.
- **Fatigue:** Feeling tired or having little energy.
- **Changes in Sleep:** Sleeping too much or too little.
- **Appetite Changes:** Significant weight loss or gain.
- **Difficulty Concentrating:** Trouble focusing or making decisions.

- **Thoughts of Death:** Recurrent thoughts of death or suicide.

Bipolar II Disorder

Bipolar II Disorder is a mental health condition characterized by mood swings that include periods of depression and hypomania. Unlike Bipolar I Disorder, Bipolar II does not involve full-blown manic episodes.

Key Features

- **Hypomanic Episodes:** These are periods of elevated mood, increased activity, and energy levels that are less intense than manic episodes. Hypomanic episodes last at least four days and do not cause significant impairment in social or occupational functioning.
- **Depressive Episodes:** Individuals with Bipolar II Disorder experience major depressive episodes, which are periods of severe depression that last at least two weeks.

Symptoms

Hypomanic Episode Symptoms:

- **Elevated Mood:** Feeling unusually happy, energetic, or irritable.
- **Increased Activity:** Engaging in multiple activities, often with less need for sleep.
- **Grandiosity:** Inflated self-esteem or unrealistic beliefs in one's abilities.
- **Rapid Speech:** Talking quickly and jumping from one topic to another.
- **Impulsivity:** Engaging in risky behaviors, such as spending sprees or reckless driving.

Depressive Episode Symptoms:

- **Persistent Sadness:** Feeling down or hopeless for most of the day.
- **Loss of Interest:** No longer finding pleasure in activities once enjoyed.
- **Fatigue:** Feeling tired or having little energy.
- **Changes in Sleep:** Sleeping too much or too little.
- **Appetite Changes:** Significant weight loss or gain.
- **Difficulty Concentrating:** Trouble focusing or making decisions.
- **Thoughts of Death:** Recurrent thoughts of death or suicide.

Cyclothymic Disorder

Cyclothymic Disorder, also known as cyclothymia, is a chronic mood disorder characterized by fluctuating periods of hypomanic and depressive symptoms that are less severe than those seen in Bipolar I or II disorders.

Key Features

- **Mood Swings:** Cyclothymic disorder involves chronic mood swings that alternate between hypomanic and depressive symptoms. These mood changes are less intense but more persistent than those in other bipolar disorders.
- **Duration:** Symptoms must be present for at least two years in adults (one year in children and adolescents) with no symptom-free periods longer than two months.

Symptoms

Hypomanic Symptoms:

- **Elevated Mood:** Feeling unusually happy, energetic, or irritable.
- **Increased Activity:** Engaging in multiple activities, often with less need for sleep.
- **Grandiosity:** Inflated self-esteem or unrealistic beliefs in one's abilities.

- **Rapid Speech:** Talking quickly and jumping from one topic to another.
- **Impulsivity:** Engaging in risky behaviors, such as spending sprees or reckless driving.

Depressive Symptoms:

- **Persistent Sadness:** Feeling down or hopeless for most of the day.
- **Loss of Interest:** No longer finding pleasure in activities once enjoyed.
- **Fatigue:** Feeling tired or having little energy.
- **Changes in Sleep:** Sleeping too much or too little.
- **Appetite Changes:** Significant weight loss or gain.
- **Difficulty Concentrating:** Trouble focusing or making decisions.
- **Feelings of Worthlessness:** Persistent feelings of guilt or worthlessness.

Soft Bipolar Disorder

Soft Bipolar Disorder, also known as subthreshold bipolar disorder, refers to a spectrum of mood disorders that exhibit some features of bipolar disorder but do not meet the full criteria for Bipolar I or II disorders. This term is not officially recognized in the Diagnostic and Statistical Manual of Mental Disorders (DSM-5), but it is used by some clinicians to describe milder forms of bipolar symptoms.

Key Features

- **Mood Swings:** Individuals with soft bipolar disorder experience mood swings that are less severe than those seen in Bipolar I or II disorders. These mood changes can include periods of elevated mood (hypomania) and periods of depression.
- **Subthreshold Symptoms:** The symptoms do not fully meet the diagnostic criteria for hypomanic or major depressive episodes but still cause significant distress or impairment.

Symptoms

Hypomanic Symptoms:

- **Elevated Mood:** Feeling unusually happy, energetic, or irritable.
- **Increased Activity:** Engaging in multiple activities, often with less need for sleep.
- **Grandiosity:** Inflated self-esteem or unrealistic beliefs in one's abilities.

- **Rapid Speech:** Talking quickly and jumping from one topic to another.
- **Impulsivity:** Engaging in risky behaviors, such as spending sprees or reckless driving.

Depressive Symptoms:

- **Persistent Sadness:** Feeling down or hopeless for most of the day.
- **Loss of Interest:** No longer finding pleasure in activities once enjoyed.
- **Fatigue:** Feeling tired or having little energy.
- **Changes in Sleep:** Sleeping too much or too little.
- **Appetite Changes:** Significant weight loss or gain.
- **Difficulty Concentrating:** Trouble focusing or making decisions.
- **Feelings of Worthlessness:** Persistent feelings of guilt or worthlessness.

Schizoaffective Disorder

Schizoaffective Disorder is a chronic mental health condition characterized by a combination of symptoms of schizophrenia and mood disorders, such as depression or mania. This disorder can significantly impact a person's thoughts, emotions, and behavior.

Key Features

- **Combination of Symptoms:** Schizoaffective disorder includes symptoms of both schizophrenia (such as hallucinations and delusions) and mood disorders (such as depressive or manic episodes).
- **Types:** There are two main types of schizoaffective disorder:
    - **Bipolar Type:** Includes episodes of mania and sometimes major depression.
    - **Depressive Type:** Includes only major depressive episodes.

Symptoms

Schizophrenia Symptoms:

- **Hallucinations:** Seeing or hearing things that aren't there.
- **Delusions:** Strongly held false beliefs that are not based in reality.
- **Disorganized Thinking:** Trouble organizing thoughts or connecting them logically.
- **Abnormal Motor Behavior:** This can range from agitation to catatonia.

Mood Disorder Symptoms:

- **Depressive Symptoms:** Persistent sadness, loss of interest in activities, changes in appetite and sleep, fatigue, feelings of worthlessness, and thoughts of death or suicide.
- **Manic Symptoms:** Elevated mood, increased energy, reduced need for sleep, grandiosity, rapid speech, and impulsive behavior.

Other Specified Bipolar and Related Disorders

Other Specified Bipolar and Related Disorders is a category in the DSM-5 (Diagnostic and Statistical Manual of Mental Disorders, Fifth Edition) used to diagnose individuals who exhibit symptoms characteristic of bipolar and related disorders but do not meet the full criteria for any specific type, such as Bipolar I, Bipolar II, or Cyclothymic Disorder. This category allows clinicians to acknowledge significant clinical impairment without fitting into the standard classifications.

Key Features

- **Subthreshold Symptoms:** Individuals have symptoms that are similar to those of bipolar disorders but do not meet the full diagnostic criteria for any specific type.
- **Clinical Significance:** Despite not meeting full criteria, the symptoms cause significant distress or impairment in social, occupational, or other important areas of functioning.

Types of Presentations

The DSM-5 outlines several specific presentations under this category:

1. **Short-Duration Hypomanic Episodes (2-3 days) and Major Depressive Episodes:**
   - Individuals experience hypomanic episodes that last only 2-3 days, which is shorter than the 4-day minimum required for Bipolar II Disorder.
   - These episodes are accompanied by major depressive episodes.
2. **Hypomanic Episodes with Insufficient Symptoms and Major Depressive Episodes:**
   - Individuals have hypomanic episodes that do not meet the full symptomatic criteria (e.g., fewer symptoms or shorter duration).
   - These episodes occur alongside major depressive episodes.

3. **Hypomanic Episode Without Prior Major Depressive Episode:**

Individuals experience one or more hypomanic episodes without ever having a major depressive episode.

This can occur in individuals with an established diagnosis of persistent depressive disorder (dysthymia).

4. **Short-Duration Cyclothymia (Less than 24 months):**

Individuals have multiple episodes of hypomanic and depressive symptoms that do not meet the criteria for hypomanic or major depressive episodes.

These symptoms persist for less than 24 months (less than 12 months for children and adolescents).

Symptoms

Hypomanic Symptoms:

- **Elevated Mood:** Feeling unusually happy, energetic, or irritable.
- **Increased Activity:** Engaging in multiple activities, often with less need for sleep.
- **Grandiosity:** Inflated self-esteem or unrealistic beliefs in one's abilities.

- **Rapid Speech:** Talking quickly and jumping from one topic to another.
- **Impulsivity:** Engaging in risky behaviors, such as spending sprees or reckless driving.

Depressive Symptoms:

- **Persistent Sadness:** Feeling down or hopeless for most of the day.
- **Loss of Interest:** No longer finding pleasure in activities once enjoyed.
- **Fatigue:** Feeling tired or having little energy.
- **Changes in Sleep:** Sleeping too much or too little.
- **Appetite Changes:** Significant weight loss or gain.
- **Difficulty Concentrating:** Trouble focusing or making decisions.
- **Feelings of Worthlessness:** Persistent feelings of guilt or worthlessness.

Chapter 4

Causes Of Bipolar Disorders

The Brain's Role

Bipolar disorder is a complex mental health condition that significantly impacts the brain's structure and function. Understanding the brain's relationship with bipolar:

Brain Structures Involved

Several key brain structures are affected by bipolar disorder:

- Prefrontal Cortex: This area is responsible for executive functions such as decision-making, impulse control, and emotional regulation. In individuals with bipolar disorder, the prefrontal cortex often shows reduced activity and structural abnormalities, which can contribute to mood swings and impulsive behavior.
- Hippocampus: The hippocampus plays a crucial role in memory formation and emotional regulation. Studies have shown that people with bipolar disorder may have a smaller

hippocampus, which can affect their ability to regulate emotions and recall information.

- Amygdala: This region is involved in processing emotions and is often hyperactive in individuals with bipolar disorder. This hyperactivity can lead to heightened emotional responses and mood instability.

Neurotransmitter Imbalances

Neurotransmitters are chemicals that transmit signals between nerve cells in the brain. Imbalances in these chemicals are closely linked to bipolar disorder:

- Serotonin: Often referred to as the "feel-good" neurotransmitter, serotonin helps regulate mood, sleep, and appetite. Low levels of serotonin are associated with depressive episodes, while imbalances can contribute to mood swings.
- Dopamine: This neurotransmitter is involved in reward and pleasure pathways. Abnormal dopamine levels can lead to the manic and hypomanic episodes characteristic of bipolar disorder.
- Norepinephrine: This neurotransmitter plays a role in the body's stress response. Imbalances in norepinephrine can affect mood and energy

levels, contributing to both manic and depressive episodes.

Structural and Functional Changes

Bipolar disorder is associated with various structural and functional changes in the brain:

- Gray Matter Reduction: Gray matter, which contains most of the brain's neuronal cell bodies, is often reduced in volume in individuals with bipolar disorder. This reduction is particularly noticeable in the prefrontal cortex and temporal lobes, affecting cognitive functions and emotional regulation.
- White Matter Abnormalities: White matter consists of nerve fibers that connect different brain regions. Abnormalities in white matter can disrupt communication between brain regions, contributing to the symptoms of bipolar disorder.

Impact on Cognitive Functions

Bipolar disorder can affect various cognitive functions, including:

- Attention and Concentration: Individuals with bipolar disorder may experience difficulties in maintaining attention and concentration, particularly during mood episodes.
- Memory: Both short-term and long-term memory can be affected, with individuals often reporting memory lapses during depressive or manic episodes.
- Executive Functioning: This includes planning, decision-making, and problem-solving abilities, which can be impaired in individuals with bipolar disorder.

Treatment and Management

Understanding the brain's relationship with bipolar disorder is crucial for effective treatment and management:

- Medication: Mood stabilizers, antipsychotics, and antidepressants can help regulate neurotransmitter levels and stabilize mood.
- Therapy: Cognitive-behavioral therapy (CBT) and other therapeutic approaches can help individuals develop coping strategies and improve cognitive functions.

- Lifestyle Changes: Regular exercise, a balanced diet, and adequate sleep can support brain health and help manage symptoms.

How the Body Handles Stress

The body's response to stress is a complex process involving various systems and mechanisms. For individuals with bipolar disorder, stress can significantly impact mood stability and overall mental health.

The Stress Response System

When the body perceives a threat or stressor, it activates the hypothalamic-pituitary-adrenal (HPA) axis. This system involves the following steps:

- Hypothalamus Activation: The hypothalamus releases corticotropin-releasing hormone (CRH).
- Pituitary Gland Response: CRH stimulates the pituitary gland to release adrenocorticotropic hormone (ACTH).
- Adrenal Glands Activation: ACTH prompts the adrenal glands to produce cortisol, the primary stress hormone.

Role of Cortisol

Cortisol helps the body manage stress by:

- Increasing Energy Availability: It raises blood sugar levels and enhances the brain's use of glucose.
- Suppressing Non-Essential Functions: It temporarily suppresses functions like digestion and immune responses to prioritize dealing with the stressor.

Stress and Bipolar Disorder

Individuals with bipolar disorder often have an altered stress response:

- Elevated Basal Cortisol Levels: People with bipolar disorder may have higher baseline levels of cortisol, even when not under acute stress.
- Blunted Stress Response: Their bodies might show a reduced ability to regulate cortisol levels after a stressor, leading to prolonged stress responses.

Impact on Mood and Episodes

Stress can trigger mood episodes in bipolar disorder:

- Manic Episodes: High stress levels can lead to increased energy, reduced need for sleep, and

heightened irritability, potentially triggering manic or hypomanic episodes.
  - Depressive Episodes: Chronic stress can deplete the body's resources, leading to feelings of hopelessness, fatigue, and depression.

Neurotransmitter Imbalances

Stress affects neurotransmitter systems, including serotonin, dopamine, and norepinephrine, which are crucial for mood regulation. Imbalances in these neurotransmitters can exacerbate bipolar symptoms.

The Role Hormones Play

The hormonal system plays a significant role in the regulation of mood and behavior, and its influence on bipolar disorder is an area of active research. Bipolar disorder is characterized by extreme mood swings, including manic and depressive episodes, and hormonal imbalances can exacerbate these symptoms.

Hormonal Imbalances and Mood Regulation

Hormones are chemical messengers that regulate numerous bodily functions, including mood, energy levels, and cognitive processes. When these delicate chemical balances are disrupted, it can lead to hormonal imbalances, which may exacerbate or even trigger bipolar symptoms.

Key Hormones Involved

Several hormones are particularly relevant to bipolar disorder:

- Cortisol: Known as the stress hormone, cortisol levels are often elevated in individuals with bipolar disorder. Chronic stress and elevated cortisol can lead to mood instability and trigger both manic and depressive episodes.
- Thyroid Hormones: Thyroid dysfunction is common in individuals with bipolar disorder. Hypothyroidism (low thyroid hormone levels) can contribute to depressive symptoms, while hyperthyroidism (high thyroid hormone levels) can exacerbate manic symptoms.
- Sex Hormones: Estrogen and progesterone fluctuations, particularly in women, can influence mood. For example, some women with bipolar disorder experience more severe mood swings during menstrual cycles, pregnancy, or menopause.

The Hypothalamic-Pituitary-Adrenal (HPA) Axis

The HPA axis is a central part of the body's stress response system and involves the interaction between the hypothalamus, pituitary gland, and adrenal glands. In individuals with bipolar disorder, the HPA axis often shows dysregulation:

- Hypothalamus: Releases corticotropin-releasing hormone (CRH) in response to stress.
- Pituitary Gland: Releases adrenocorticotropic hormone (ACTH) in response to CRH.
- Adrenal Glands: Produce cortisol in response to ACTH[2].

Dysregulation of the HPA axis can lead to abnormal cortisol levels, contributing to mood swings and stress sensitivity in bipolar disorder.

Hormonal Changes and Mood Episodes

Hormonal fluctuations can act as triggers for mood episodes in bipolar disorder:

- Menstrual Cycle: Hormonal changes during the menstrual cycle can lead to increased mood instability in women with bipolar disorder.
- Pregnancy and Postpartum Period: Significant hormonal shifts during and after pregnancy can trigger mood episodes.
- Menopause: Hormonal changes during menopause can exacerbate bipolar symptoms.

Inflammatory and Immune Responses

Hormones also interact with the immune system, and inflammation has been linked to mood disorders. Elevated levels of inflammatory markers, such as C-reactive protein (CRP), have been observed in individuals with bipolar disorder, suggesting a link between hormonal imbalances, inflammation, and mood regulation.

Chronobiology

Circadian Rhythms And Bipolar Disorder

Circadian rhythms are natural, internal processes that regulate the sleep-wake cycle and repeat roughly every 24 hours. These rhythms are crucial for maintaining various physiological functions, including hormone release, body temperature, and sleep patterns. In individuals with bipolar disorder, disruptions in circadian rhythms can significantly impact mood stability and overall mental health.

Understanding Circadian Rhythms

Circadian rhythms are controlled by the suprachiasmatic nucleus (SCN), a group of cells located in the hypothalamus. The SCN acts as the body's master clock, synchronizing various biological processes with the external environment, primarily through light exposure.

Circadian Rhythms and Bipolar Disorder

Research has shown that individuals with bipolar disorder often experience significant disruptions in their circadian rhythms. These disruptions can manifest in several ways:

- Sleep-Wake Cycle: People with bipolar disorder frequently have irregular sleep patterns, including insomnia, hypersomnia (excessive sleep), and altered sleep architecture. These irregularities can trigger or exacerbate mood episodes.
- Body Temperature: Circadian rhythms also regulate body temperature, which tends to fluctuate throughout the day. In bipolar disorder, these fluctuations can be more pronounced, contributing to mood instability.
- Hormonal Cycles: Hormones such as cortisol and melatonin follow circadian patterns.

Disruptions in these hormonal cycles can affect mood regulation and stress responses in individuals with bipolar disorder.

The Role of Clock Genes

Clock genes are responsible for maintaining circadian rhythms at the molecular level. Variations or mutations in these genes can disrupt the normal functioning of the circadian system. Studies have identified several clock genes, such as **CLOCK** and **BMAL1**, that are associated with bipolar disorder. These genetic variations can lead to altered circadian rhythms and increased susceptibility to mood episodes.

Impact on Mood Episodes

Disruptions in circadian rhythms can have a profound impact on mood episodes in bipolar disorder:

- Manic Episodes: Irregular sleep patterns and reduced need for sleep are common during manic episodes. These disruptions can further destabilize circadian rhythms, creating a vicious cycle that exacerbates mania.
- Depressive Episodes: Conversely, depressive episodes are often characterized by hypersomnia and difficulty maintaining a regular sleep schedule. These changes can disrupt

circadian rhythms and prolong depressive symptoms.

Genetics And Bipolar Disorder

Genetics plays a significant role in the development of bipolar disorder, although it is not the sole factor.

Genetic Predisposition

- Family History: Bipolar disorder tends to run in families, indicating a genetic predisposition. If a close relative, such as a parent or sibling, has bipolar disorder, the risk of developing the condition is higher.
- Twin Studies: Studies involving twins have shown that if one identical twin has bipolar disorder, the other twin has a 40-70% chance of developing the condition, compared to a 5-10% chance in non-identical twins.

Specific Genes and Genetic Variations

- Polygenic Nature: Bipolar disorder is polygenic, meaning multiple genes contribute to its development. No single gene causes the disorder; instead, several genetic variations collectively increase the risk.

- Genome-Wide Association Studies (GWAS): GWAS have identified several genetic loci associated with bipolar disorder. These studies have highlighted regions on chromosomes 4p16, 12q23-q24, 16p13, 21q22, and Xq24-q26 as areas of interest.
- Candidate Genes: Some specific genes, such as CACNA1C, ANK3, and CLOCK, have been implicated in bipolar disorder. These genes are involved in regulating neurotransmitter systems and circadian rhythms, which are crucial for mood regulation.

Genetic Mechanisms

- Epistasis: This refers to the interaction between different genes. In bipolar disorder, multiple genes may interact in complex ways to influence susceptibility.
- Dynamic Mutation and Imprinting: These are more complex genetic mechanisms that may also play a role in the development of bipolar disorder. Dynamic mutations involve changes in the number of repeats in certain DNA sequences, while imprinting refers to the

differential expression of genes depending on their parental origin.

Heritability

- Heritability Estimates: The heritability of bipolar disorder is estimated to be between 60-85%, indicating a strong genetic component. This means that a significant portion of the risk for developing bipolar disorder can be attributed to genetic factors.
- Environmental Interactions: While genetics play a crucial role, environmental factors also contribute to the development of bipolar disorder. Stressful life events, substance abuse, and other environmental factors can interact with genetic predispositions to trigger mood episodes.

Chapter 5

Treatments

Meditation

Meditation is a powerful tool for stabilizing mood and managing mental health conditions, including bipolar disorder. It involves practices that promote relaxation, mindfulness, and a heightened state of awareness.

Understanding Meditation

Meditation encompasses a variety of practices aimed at focusing the mind and achieving a state of calm and clarity. Common forms of meditation include:

- Mindfulness Meditation: Involves paying attention to the present moment without judgment. It helps in recognizing and accepting thoughts and feelings as they arise.
- Transcendental Meditation: Uses a mantra or repeated word/phrase to help the mind settle into a state of restful alertness.
- Loving-Kindness Meditation: Focuses on developing feelings of compassion and love towards oneself and others.

Benefits of Meditation for Mood Stabilization

Meditation offers several benefits that can help stabilize mood:

- Reduces Stress: Meditation activates the parasympathetic nervous system, promoting relaxation and reducing the body's stress response.
- Enhances Emotional Regulation: Regular meditation practice can improve the ability to manage and respond to emotions, reducing the intensity of mood swings.
- Improves Sleep: Meditation can help regulate sleep patterns, which is crucial for mood stability, especially in individuals with bipolar disorder.
- Increases Mindfulness: Being more mindful helps individuals recognize early signs of mood changes and implement coping strategies before symptoms escalate.

Meditation Techniques for Mood Stabilization

Several meditation techniques are particularly effective for stabilizing mood:

- Mindfulness-Based Cognitive Therapy (MBCT): Combines mindfulness practices with cognitive therapy techniques to prevent relapse in depression and manage mood swings.

- Breathing Exercises: Simple breathing techniques, such as deep breathing or diaphragmatic breathing, can quickly reduce stress and promote a sense of calm.
- Body Scan Meditation: Involves focusing attention on different parts of the body, promoting relaxation and awareness of physical sensations.

Scientific Evidence

Research supports the effectiveness of meditation in stabilizing mood and managing mental health conditions:

- Reduced Anxiety and Depression: Studies have shown that mindfulness meditation can significantly reduce symptoms of anxiety and depression.
- Improved Brain Function: Meditation has been found to increase gray matter in brain regions associated with emotional regulation and self-control.
- Lower Cortisol Levels: Regular meditation practice can reduce cortisol levels, the body's primary stress hormone, contributing to overall mood stability.

Practical Tips for Starting Meditation

For those new to meditation, here are some practical tips to get started:

- Start Small: Begin with short sessions, such as 5-10 minutes, and gradually increase the duration as you become more comfortable.
- Find a Quiet Space: Choose a quiet, comfortable place where you won't be disturbed.
- Use Guided Meditations: Guided meditation apps or videos can provide structure and support, especially for beginners.
- Be Consistent: Regular practice is key to experiencing the benefits of meditation. Aim to meditate at the same time each day.

Mood Stabilizing Medications

Mood stabilizing medications are essential in the treatment of bipolar disorder and other mental health conditions characterized by mood swings. These medications help manage the highs (mania) and lows (depression) associated with these conditions.

Types of Mood Stabilizers

Mood stabilizers can be broadly categorized into three main types: lithium, anticonvulsants, and antipsychotics.

a. Lithium

- Overview: Lithium is one of the oldest and most well-known mood stabilizers. It has been used for over 70 years and is considered a first-line treatment for bipolar disorder.
- Mechanism of Action: Lithium works by affecting the flow of sodium through nerve and muscle cells, which influences the release of neurotransmitters and stabilizes mood.
- Common Brands: Eskalith®, Lithobid®, Priadel, Camcolit.
- Side Effects: Common side effects include increased thirst, hand tremors, and frequent urination. High levels of lithium in the blood can be toxic, so regular blood tests are necessary to monitor levels.

b. Anticonvulsants

- Overview: Originally developed to treat epilepsy, anticonvulsants are also effective mood stabilizers. They help manage mood swings by reducing abnormal electrical activity in the brain.

- Common Medications:
    - Valproate (Depakote®): Effective for treating manic episodes and preventing future episodes.
    - Lamotrigine (Lamictal®): Particularly effective for preventing depressive episodes in bipolar disorder.
    - Carbamazepine (Tegretol®): Used for treating acute mania and preventing future episodes.
- Side Effects: Side effects can include dizziness, drowsiness, weight gain, and gastrointestinal issues. Regular monitoring is necessary to manage potential side effects..

c. Antipsychotics

- Overview: Antipsychotic medications are often used in combination with other mood stabilizers to manage severe mood swings and psychotic symptoms.
- Common Medications:
    - Aripiprazole (Abilify®): Used to treat manic and mixed episodes.
    - Quetiapine (Seroquel®): Effective for treating both manic and depressive episodes.

- Olanzapine (Zyprexa®): Used for acute mania and maintenance therapy.
- Side Effects: Side effects can include weight gain, metabolic changes, and sedation. Regular monitoring is essential to manage these effects.

Mechanism of Action

Mood stabilizers work by affecting neurotransmitter systems in the brain, including serotonin, dopamine, and norepinephrine. They help balance these chemicals, reducing abnormal brain activity and stabilizing mood.

Uses Beyond Bipolar Disorder

While primarily used to treat bipolar disorder, mood stabilizers are also prescribed for other mental health conditions, including:

- Major Depressive Disorder: To manage treatment-resistant depression.
- Schizoaffective Disorder: To stabilize mood and reduce psychotic symptoms.
- Borderline Personality Disorder: To manage mood swings and impulsivity.
- Post-Traumatic Stress Disorder (PTSD): To reduce mood instability and anxiety.

Monitoring and Management

Regular monitoring is crucial when taking mood stabilizers to ensure effectiveness and manage side effects:

- Blood Tests: Regular blood tests are necessary for medications like lithium and valproate to monitor levels and prevent toxicity.
- Physical Health Monitoring: Monitoring weight, blood pressure, and metabolic health is essential, especially for antipsychotic medications.
- Mental Health Assessments: Regular check-ins with a healthcare provider to assess mood stability and adjust treatment as needed.

Antidepressant Medications

Antidepressant medications are commonly used to treat depression and other mental health conditions. They work by altering the levels of neurotransmitters in the brain, which are chemicals that affect mood and emotions.

Types of Antidepressants

Antidepressants are classified into several categories based on their chemical structure and mechanism of action:

a. Selective Serotonin Reuptake Inhibitors (SSRIs)

- Overview: SSRIs are the most commonly prescribed antidepressants. They work by increasing the levels of serotonin, a neurotransmitter associated with mood regulation, in the brain.
- Common Medications: Fluoxetine (Prozac®), Sertraline (Zoloft®), Citalopram (Celexa®), Escitalopram (Lexapro®), Paroxetine (Paxil®).
- Side Effects: Nausea, insomnia, sexual dysfunction, and weight gain.

b. Serotonin-Norepinephrine Reuptake Inhibitors (SNRIs)

- Overview: SNRIs increase the levels of both serotonin and norepinephrine, another neurotransmitter involved in mood regulation.
- Common Medications: Venlafaxine (Effexor®), Duloxetine (Cymbalta®), Desvenlafaxine (Pristiq®), Levomilnacipran (Fetzima®).
- Side Effects: Nausea, dry mouth, dizziness, and increased blood pressure.

c. Atypical Antidepressants

- Overview: This category includes medications that do not fit neatly into other classes. They work through various mechanisms to affect neurotransmitter levels.
- Common Medications: Bupropion (Wellbutrin®), Mirtazapine (Remeron®), Trazodone (Desyrel®), Vortioxetine (Trintellix®), Vilazodone (Viibryd®).
- Side Effects: Vary depending on the medication but can include dry mouth, drowsiness, and weight gain.

d. Tricyclic Antidepressants (TCAs)

- Overview: TCAs are older antidepressants that work by blocking the reuptake of serotonin and norepinephrine.
- Common Medications: Amitriptyline (Elavil®), Nortriptyline (Pamelor®), Imipramine (Tofranil®), Doxepin (Sinequan®), Desipramine (Norpram®)
- Side Effects: Dry mouth, blurred vision, constipation, urinary retention, and weight gain.

e. Monoamine Oxidase Inhibitors (MAOIs)

- Overview: MAOIs work by inhibiting the enzyme monoamine oxidase, which breaks down neurotransmitters like serotonin, norepinephrine, and dopamine.

- Common Medications: Phenelzine (Nardil®), Tranylcypromine (Parnate®), Isocarboxazid (Marplan®), Selegiline (Emsam®).
- Side Effects: Dietary restrictions are necessary to avoid hypertensive crises. Other side effects include dizziness, insomnia, and weight gain.

Mechanism of Action

Antidepressants work by altering the balance of neurotransmitters in the brain. Each class of antidepressants affects different neurotransmitters and their pathways:

- SSRIs: Block the reuptake of serotonin, increasing its availability in the synaptic cleft.
- SNRIs: Block the reuptake of both serotonin and norepinephrine.
- Atypical Antidepressants: Vary in their mechanisms, affecting different neurotransmitters.
- TCAs: Block the reuptake of serotonin and norepinephrine, and also affect other neurotransmitter systems.
- MAOIs: Inhibit the enzyme monoamine oxidase, preventing the breakdown of neurotransmitters.

Uses of Antidepressants

While primarily used to treat depression, antidepressants are also prescribed for other conditions, including:

- Anxiety Disorders: Generalized anxiety disorder, panic disorder, social anxiety disorder.
- Obsessive-Compulsive Disorder (OCD): SSRIs are commonly used to manage OCD symptoms.
- Post-Traumatic Stress Disorder (PTSD): Antidepressants can help manage symptoms of PTSD.
- Chronic Pain: Certain antidepressants, particularly SNRIs and TCAs, are effective in managing chronic pain conditions like fibromyalgia and neuropathic pain.
- Eating Disorders: Antidepressants can be used to treat bulimia nervosa and binge-eating disorder.

Considerations and Side Effects

When prescribing antidepressants, healthcare providers consider several factors:

- Side Effects: Each class of antidepressants has its own side effect profile. Patients should be monitored for adverse effects and dosage adjustments may be necessary.

- Drug Interactions: Antidepressants can interact with other medications, so a thorough review of the patient's medication history is essential.
- Response Time: Antidepressants typically take several weeks to show their full effect. Patients should be informed about this delay to manage expectations.
- Discontinuation Syndrome: Abruptly stopping antidepressants can lead to withdrawal symptoms. Gradual tapering is recommended under medical supervision.

Pipeline Drugs For Bipolar Disorders

The development of new medications for bipolar disorder is an ongoing area of research, with several promising drugs currently in the pipeline. These drugs aim to improve the treatment of bipolar disorder by offering better efficacy, fewer side effects, and novel mechanisms of action.

Lumateperone (Caplyta)

- Overview: Lumateperone is an atypical antipsychotic developed by Intra-Cellular

Therapies. It is currently in the pre-registration stage for the treatment of depressive episodes associated with bipolar I and II disorder.

- Mechanism of Action: Lumateperone acts on multiple neurotransmitter systems, including serotonin, dopamine, and glutamate receptors. This multi-target approach helps in stabilizing mood and reducing depressive symptoms.
- Clinical Trials: Clinical trials have shown that lumateperone is effective as both monotherapy and adjunctive therapy with lithium or valproate. It has demonstrated a favorable safety profile with fewer metabolic side effects compared to other antipsychotics.

NRX-100/NRX-101

- Overview: Developed by NeuroRx, Inc., NRX-100/NRX-101 is a combination therapy designed to treat acute suicidal ideation and behavior in bipolar depression.
- Mechanism of Action: NRX-100 is an intravenous formulation of ketamine, which provides rapid relief from depressive symptoms. NRX-101 is an oral formulation of D-cycloserine and lurasidone, which helps maintain the antidepressant effects and prevent relapse.

- Clinical Trials: Early clinical trials have shown promising results in reducing suicidal ideation and improving depressive symptoms. The combination therapy is currently in advanced stages of clinical development.

Zuranolone (SAGE-217)

- Overview: Zuranolone is an oral neuroactive steroid developed by Sage Therapeutics. It is being investigated for the treatment of major depressive disorder and bipolar depression.
- Mechanism of Action: Zuranolone modulates GABA-A receptors, enhancing inhibitory neurotransmission in the brain. This helps in stabilizing mood and reducing symptoms of depression.
- Clinical Trials: Clinical trials have demonstrated rapid and sustained antidepressant effects with zuranolone. It is currently in phase 3 clinical trials for bipolar depression.

SEP-856 (SEP-363856)

- Overview: SEP-856 is a novel psychotropic agent developed by Sunovion Pharmaceuticals. It is being investigated for the treatment of schizophrenia and bipolar disorder.

- Mechanism of Action: SEP-856 acts as a trace amine-associated receptor 1 (TAAR-1) agonist and a serotonin 5-HT1A receptor agonist. This dual mechanism helps in modulating neurotransmitter systems involved in mood regulation.
- Clinical Trials: Early clinical trials have shown efficacy in reducing both positive and negative symptoms of schizophrenia, with potential applications in bipolar disorder. It is currently in phase 2 clinical trials.

Esketamine (Falkieri)

- Overview: Esketamine is a nasal spray formulation developed by Celon Pharma. It is being investigated for the treatment of treatment-resistant bipolar depression.
- Mechanism of Action: Esketamine is an NMDA receptor antagonist, which helps in rapidly reducing depressive symptoms by modulating glutamate neurotransmission.
- Clinical Trials: Phase 2 clinical trials have shown positive results in reducing depressive symptoms in patients with treatment-resistant bipolar depression. It is currently in further stages of clinical development.

Importance Of A Diet

Diet plays a crucial role in managing bipolar disorder by supporting overall brain health, stabilizing mood, and reducing the risk of mood swings. While there is no specific diet for bipolar disorder, certain foods and dietary patterns can help manage symptoms and improve well-being.

Importance of a Balanced Diet

A balanced diet provides essential nutrients that support brain function and overall health. Key components of a balanced diet include:

- Fruits and Vegetables: Rich in vitamins, minerals, and antioxidants, fruits and vegetables help reduce inflammation and support brain health.
- Whole Grains: Whole grains like brown rice, quinoa, and oats provide a steady source of energy and help regulate blood sugar levels, which can affect mood.
- Lean Proteins: Sources like chicken, fish, beans, and legumes provide essential amino acids that are necessary for neurotransmitter production.

- Healthy Fats: Omega-3 fatty acids found in fish, flaxseeds, and walnuts are particularly beneficial for brain health and mood regulation.

Foods to Include

Certain foods have been shown to have positive effects on mood and brain function:

- Omega-3 Fatty Acids: Found in fatty fish (salmon, mackerel, sardines), flaxseeds, chia seeds, and walnuts, omega-3s have anti-inflammatory properties and support brain health.
- Probiotics: Foods like yogurt, kefir, sauerkraut, and kimchi support gut health, which is linked to mood regulation through the gut-brain axis.
- Magnesium-Rich Foods: Magnesium helps regulate neurotransmitters and can be found in leafy greens, nuts, seeds, and whole grains.
- Vitamin D: Found in fatty fish, fortified dairy products, and exposure to sunlight, vitamin D is important for mood regulation.
- Tryptophan-Rich Foods: Tryptophan is an amino acid that helps produce serotonin, a neurotransmitter that regulates mood. Foods rich in tryptophan include turkey, chicken, tofu, eggs, and cheese.

Foods to Avoid

Certain foods can exacerbate symptoms of bipolar disorder and should be limited or avoided:

- Alcohol: Alcohol can interfere with medications and exacerbate mood swings.
- Caffeine: Excessive caffeine intake can lead to increased anxiety and disrupt sleep patterns, which are crucial for mood stability.
- Sugar and Refined Carbohydrates: High sugar intake can lead to blood sugar spikes and crashes, affecting mood and energy levels.
- Processed Foods: Foods high in trans fats, preservatives, and artificial additives can negatively impact brain health and mood.

Hydration

Staying hydrated is essential for overall health and can help manage symptoms of bipolar disorder. Drinking plenty of water and limiting sugary drinks and caffeine can support mood stability.

Meal Timing and Regularity

Regular meal timing helps maintain stable blood sugar levels, which can influence mood. Eating small, balanced meals throughout the day can prevent mood swings and provide consistent energy.

Supplements

In some cases, dietary supplements may be recommended to ensure adequate intake of essential nutrients:

- Omega-3 Supplements: For those who do not consume enough omega-3s through diet, supplements can be beneficial.
- Vitamin D Supplements: Especially important for individuals with limited sun exposure.
- Magnesium Supplements: Can help support neurotransmitter function and mood regulation.

Alcohol And Drug Abuse

Drug abuse and alcohol use are significant concerns for individuals with bipolar disorder. The co-occurrence of substance use disorders and bipolar disorder can complicate treatment and worsen symptoms.

Prevalence and Co-occurrence

- High Prevalence: Individuals with bipolar disorder are at a higher risk of developing substance use disorders compared to the general population. Studies suggest that up to

60% of people with bipolar disorder will experience a substance use disorder at some point in their lives.
- Dual Diagnosis: When a person has both bipolar disorder and a substance use disorder, it is referred to as a dual diagnosis. This combination can make each condition more severe and harder to treat.

Reasons for Co-occurrence

Several factors contribute to the high co-occurrence of bipolar disorder and substance use disorders:

- Self-Medication: Individuals with bipolar disorder may use drugs or alcohol to self-medicate and alleviate symptoms of mania or depression. However, this often leads to a worsening of symptoms over time.
- Genetic Factors: Genetic predispositions can increase the risk of both bipolar disorder and substance use disorders. Shared genetic factors may influence brain chemistry and behavior.
- Neurotransmitter Imbalances: Both conditions involve dysregulation of neurotransmitters such as dopamine, serotonin, and norepinephrine, which play crucial roles in mood regulation and reward pathways.

- Environmental Stressors: Stressful life events, trauma, and social factors can trigger both bipolar episodes and substance use.

Impact of Substance Use on Bipolar Disorder

Substance use can have several negative effects on individuals with bipolar disorder:

- Worsening Symptoms: Alcohol and drug use can exacerbate symptoms of both mania and depression, leading to more frequent and severe mood episodes.
- Treatment Interference: Substance use can interfere with the effectiveness of medications used to treat bipolar disorder, making it harder to achieve mood stability.
- Increased Risk of Suicide: The combination of bipolar disorder and substance use increases the risk of suicidal thoughts and behaviors.
- Impaired Judgment: Substance use can impair judgment and lead to risky behaviors, which are already a concern during manic episodes.

Common Substances of Abuse

Individuals with bipolar disorder may misuse various substances, including:

- Alcohol: Alcohol is commonly used to self-medicate, but it can worsen depressive symptoms and disrupt sleep patterns.
- Stimulants: Drugs like cocaine and methamphetamine can trigger manic episodes and increase impulsivity.
- Opioids: Opioid misuse can lead to severe depressive symptoms and increase the risk of overdose.
- Cannabis: While some individuals use cannabis to alleviate symptoms, it can also trigger mood swings and psychosis.

Brain Stimulation Treatments

Brain stimulation treatments are emerging as promising options for managing bipolar disorder, particularly for individuals who do not respond well to traditional medications or therapies. These treatments involve using electrical or magnetic stimulation to modulate brain activity and improve mood stability.

Electroconvulsive Therapy (ECT)

- Overview: ECT is one of the oldest and most effective brain stimulation treatments for severe mood disorders, including bipolar disorder. It involves passing small electric currents through the brain to induce controlled seizures.
- Mechanism of Action: The exact mechanism is not fully understood, but ECT is believed to alter brain chemistry, leading to rapid improvements in mood.
- Procedure: ECT is typically administered under general anesthesia, with treatments given two to three times a week for several weeks.
- Efficacy: ECT is highly effective for treating severe depressive and manic episodes, particularly in treatment-resistant cases.
- Side Effects: Common side effects include short-term memory loss, confusion, and muscle aches. These side effects are usually temporary.

Transcranial Magnetic Stimulation (TMS)

- Overview: TMS is a non-invasive treatment that uses magnetic fields to stimulate nerve cells in the brain. It is primarily used to treat depression but has shown promise for bipolar disorder as well.

- Mechanism of Action: TMS targets specific brain regions involved in mood regulation, such as the prefrontal cortex, by delivering magnetic pulses that modulate neuronal activity.
- Procedure: TMS sessions are typically conducted five times a week for several weeks. Each session lasts about 30-40 minutes.
- Efficacy: Studies have shown that TMS can reduce depressive symptoms in individuals with bipolar disorder, particularly those with treatment-resistant depression.
- Side Effects: TMS is generally well-tolerated, with mild side effects such as headache, scalp discomfort, and tingling sensations.

Accelerated Intermittent Theta Burst Stimulation (aiTBS)

- Overview: aiTBS is a newer form of TMS that delivers magnetic pulses in short, rapid bursts. It has been shown to be effective in treating depression and is being explored for bipolar disorder.
- Mechanism of Action: aiTBS targets the same brain regions as traditional TMS but uses a different pattern of stimulation to achieve faster results.

- Procedure: aiTBS sessions are shorter than traditional TMS, typically lasting about 3-10 minutes, and can be administered multiple times a day over a shorter treatment period.
- Efficacy: Recent studies have shown that aiTBS can significantly reduce depressive symptoms in individuals with treatment-resistant bipolar disorder.
- Side Effects: Similar to TMS, aiTBS is well-tolerated with minimal side effects.

Vagus Nerve Stimulation (VNS)

- Overview: VNS involves implanting a device that stimulates the vagus nerve, which connects the brain to various organs in the body. It is used as an adjunctive treatment for depression and bipolar disorder.
- Mechanism of Action: VNS is thought to influence brain regions involved in mood regulation by modulating neurotransmitter levels.
- Procedure: The device is surgically implanted under the skin in the chest, with a wire connecting it to the vagus nerve in the neck. The device sends regular electrical pulses to the nerve.

- Efficacy: VNS has shown promise in reducing depressive symptoms in individuals with treatment-resistant bipolar disorder.
- Side Effects: Common side effects include hoarseness, throat pain, and coughing. These side effects often diminish over time.

Deep Brain Stimulation (DBS)

- Overview: DBS involves surgically implanting electrodes in specific brain regions to deliver continuous electrical stimulation. It is primarily used for movement disorders but is being explored for bipolar disorder.
- Mechanism of Action: DBS targets brain regions involved in mood regulation, such as the subgenual cingulate cortex, to modulate neuronal activity and improve mood stability.
- Procedure: The electrodes are connected to a pulse generator implanted under the skin in the chest. The device sends electrical impulses to the brain.
- Efficacy: Early studies suggest that DBS may be effective in reducing symptoms of treatment-resistant bipolar disorder.
- Side Effects: Potential side effects include infection, bleeding, and hardware-related

complications. Regular follow-up is necessary to adjust the device settings.

Importance Of Psychotherapy

Psychotherapy, often referred to as "talk therapy," is a crucial component in the treatment of bipolar disorder. It complements medication by addressing the psychological, social, and behavioral aspects of the disorder.

Understanding Psychotherapy

Psychotherapy involves structured sessions with a trained mental health professional, where individuals can explore their thoughts, feelings, and behaviors. It provides a safe space to discuss challenges and develop strategies for managing symptoms.

Types of Psychotherapy for Bipolar Disorder

Several types of psychotherapy have been found effective in treating bipolar disorder:

a. Cognitive-Behavioral Therapy (CBT)

- Overview: CBT focuses on identifying and changing negative thought patterns and behaviors that contribute to mood swings.
- Techniques: Techniques include cognitive restructuring, behavioral activation, and problem-solving skills.
- Benefits: CBT helps individuals recognize early signs of mood episodes, develop coping strategies, and improve emotional regulation.

b. Interpersonal and Social Rhythm Therapy (IPSRT)

- Overview: IPSRT combines interpersonal therapy with techniques to stabilize daily routines and social rhythms.
- Techniques: Emphasis is placed on maintaining regular sleep patterns, meal times, and social activities.
- Benefits: IPSRT helps reduce the frequency and severity of mood episodes by promoting stability in daily life.

c. Family-Focused Therapy (FFT)

- Overview: FFT involves family members in the treatment process to improve communication and support.

- Techniques: Techniques include psychoeducation, communication enhancement training, and problem-solving skills.
- Benefits: FFT helps families understand bipolar disorder, reduces family stress, and improves treatment adherence.

d. Psychoeducation

- Overview: Psychoeducation involves teaching individuals and their families about bipolar disorder, its symptoms, and treatment options.
- Techniques: Group sessions, workshops, and educational materials are commonly used.
- Benefits: Increases awareness, reduces stigma, and empowers individuals to manage their condition more effectively.

Benefits of Psychotherapy for Bipolar Disorder

Psychotherapy offers numerous benefits for individuals with bipolar disorder:

- Symptom Management: Helps individuals recognize early warning signs of mood episodes and develop strategies to manage symptoms.
- Medication Adherence: Encourages adherence to medication regimens by addressing concerns and misconceptions about treatment.

- Emotional Regulation: Teaches skills to manage intense emotions and reduce impulsive behaviors.
- Stress Reduction: Provides tools to cope with stress, which can trigger mood episodes.
- Improved Relationships: Enhances communication and problem-solving skills, improving relationships with family and friends.
- Enhanced Quality of Life: Supports overall well-being by promoting healthy lifestyle choices and self-care practices.

Integrating Psychotherapy with Medication

While medication is essential for stabilizing mood in bipolar disorder, psychotherapy addresses the psychological and social aspects of the condition. The combination of both approaches leads to more comprehensive and effective treatment.

Finding the Right Therapist

Finding a therapist who specializes in bipolar disorder is crucial for effective treatment. Considerations include:

- Experience: Look for therapists with experience in treating bipolar disorder and using evidence-based therapies.

- Comfort: Choose a therapist with whom you feel comfortable and can build a trusting relationship.
- Approach: Ensure the therapist's approach aligns with your treatment goals and preferences.

Chapter 6

Beginning To Thrive

Confronting And Accepting The Illness

Confronting and accepting a diagnosis of bipolar disorder can be a challenging and emotional journey. However, acceptance is a crucial step towards effective management and improved quality of life.

Understanding the Diagnosis

- Educate Yourself: Learn about bipolar disorder, its symptoms, causes, and treatment options. Understanding the condition can help demystify it and reduce fear and stigma.
- Ask Questions: Don't hesitate to ask your healthcare provider questions about your diagnosis. Understanding the specifics of your condition can help you feel more in control.

Emotional Reactions

- Acknowledge Your Feelings: It's normal to experience a range of emotions, including shock, denial, anger, sadness, and fear.

Acknowledge these feelings as a natural part of the acceptance process.
- Seek Support: Talk to trusted friends, family members, or a therapist about your feelings. Sharing your emotions can provide relief and help you feel less isolated.

Building a Support System

- Family and Friends: Surround yourself with supportive people who understand your condition and can offer encouragement and assistance.
- Support Groups: Join support groups for individuals with bipolar disorder. Connecting with others who have similar experiences can provide valuable insights and emotional support.
- Professional Help: Regularly see a mental health professional who can provide therapy and guidance as you navigate your diagnosis.

Developing a Treatment Plan

- Medication: Work with your healthcare provider to find the right medication regimen. Medication can help stabilize mood and manage symptoms.
- Therapy: Engage in therapy, such as cognitive-behavioral therapy (CBT) or interpersonal and social rhythm therapy (IPSRT), to develop

coping strategies and improve emotional
regulation.

- Lifestyle Changes: Adopt a healthy lifestyle, including regular exercise, a balanced diet, and adequate sleep. These changes can support overall well-being and mood stability.

Setting Realistic Goals

- Short-Term Goals: Set achievable short-term goals that focus on managing symptoms and improving daily functioning.
- Long-Term Goals: Establish long-term goals that align with your values and aspirations. These goals can provide motivation and a sense of purpose.

Practicing Self-Compassion

- Be Kind to Yourself: Recognize that managing bipolar disorder is a journey with ups and downs. Be patient and compassionate with yourself as you navigate this process.
- Celebrate Progress: Acknowledge and celebrate your achievements, no matter how small. Progress is progress, and every step forward is significant.

Learning to Manage Triggers

- Identify Triggers: Work with your therapist to identify triggers that can lead to mood episodes. Common triggers include stress, lack of sleep, and substance use.
- Develop Coping Strategies: Create a plan to manage triggers, such as practicing relaxation techniques, maintaining a regular routine, and avoiding alcohol and drugs.

Planning for Relapses

- Crisis Plan: Develop a crisis plan that outlines steps to take if symptoms worsen. This plan should include emergency contacts, treatment preferences, and safety measures.
- Early Intervention: Recognize early warning signs of mood episodes and seek help promptly to prevent escalation.

Advocating for Yourself

- Communicate Needs: Clearly communicate your needs and boundaries to others. Advocacy can help you receive the support and accommodations you need.
- Educate Others: Educate friends, family, and colleagues about bipolar disorder to reduce stigma and promote understanding.

Importance of Mood Hygiene

Mood hygiene refers to habits and practices that help maintain stable mood states and overall mental well-being. For individuals with bipolar disorder, mood hygiene is particularly important as it can help manage mood swings and reduce the frequency and severity of mood episodes.

Establishing a Routine

- Consistent Schedule: Maintaining a regular daily routine helps stabilize circadian rhythms, which are often disrupted in bipolar disorder. This includes consistent wake-up and bedtimes, meal times, and activity schedules.
- Sleep Hygiene: Prioritize good sleep hygiene by creating a restful sleep environment, avoiding caffeine and electronics before bed, and sticking to a regular sleep schedule.

Healthy Lifestyle Choices

- Balanced Diet: Eating a balanced diet rich in fruits, vegetables, whole grains, lean proteins, and healthy fats supports overall brain health and mood stability.

- Regular Exercise: Physical activity releases endorphins, which can improve mood and reduce stress. Aim for at least 30 minutes of moderate exercise most days of the week.
- Hydration: Staying hydrated is essential for overall health and can help manage mood swings.

Stress Management

- Relaxation Techniques: Incorporate relaxation techniques such as deep breathing, meditation, and yoga into your daily routine to reduce stress and promote relaxation.
- Time Management: Effective time management can help reduce stress by ensuring that tasks are completed in a timely manner and preventing feelings of being overwhelmed.
- Mindfulness: Practicing mindfulness can help you stay present and reduce anxiety about the future or regrets about the past.

Social Connections

- Support Network: Maintain strong social connections with friends, family, and support groups. Social support is crucial for emotional well-being and can provide a sense of belonging and understanding.

- Communication: Open and honest communication with loved ones about your condition and needs can help them provide better support and reduce misunderstandings.

Medication and Therapy Adherence

- Medication Routine: Take medications as prescribed and use tools like pill organizers or alarms to help remember doses.
- Therapy Participation: Regularly attend therapy sessions and actively engage in therapeutic activities and homework assignments.

Monitoring Mood and Symptoms

- Mood Tracking: Keep a mood diary to track mood changes, triggers, and patterns. This can help you and your healthcare provider make informed decisions about your treatment.
- Early Intervention: Recognize early warning signs of mood episodes and seek help promptly to prevent escalation.

Avoiding Substance Abuse

- Limit Alcohol: Avoid alcohol as it can interfere with medications and exacerbate mood swings.

- Avoid Drugs: Refrain from using recreational drugs, which can destabilize mood and lead to substance use disorders.

Personal Hygiene

- Daily Hygiene Routine: Maintain a daily hygiene routine, even when feeling low. Personal hygiene can impact self-esteem and overall well-being.
- Simplify Tasks: If feeling overwhelmed, simplify hygiene tasks by breaking them into smaller steps or using products that make the process easier.

Supporting Someone With Bipolar Disorder

Supporting someone with bipolar disorder can be challenging but also incredibly rewarding. Your support can make a significant difference in their treatment and overall well-being.

Educate Yourself

- Learn About Bipolar Disorder: Understanding the symptoms, treatment options, and challenges associated with bipolar disorder can help you provide better support. Knowledge about the condition can also reduce frustration and improve empathy.

- Stay Updated: Keep up with the latest research and treatment advancements to better understand what your loved one is experiencing.

Encourage Treatment

- Seek Professional Help: Encourage your loved one to seek help from a mental health professional. Early intervention can improve the prognosis.
- Support Medication Adherence: Remind them to take their medications as prescribed and attend regular check-ups. Medication is crucial for managing bipolar disorder.
- Therapy Participation: Encourage participation in therapy sessions, such as cognitive-behavioral therapy (CBT) or family-focused therapy (FFT), which can provide additional support and coping strategies.

Be a Good Listener

- Active Listening: Listen without judgment and validate their feelings. Sometimes, just being there to listen can make a significant difference.

- Avoid Dismissal: Don't dismiss their emotions or attribute all their feelings to the disorder. They may have valid concerns and feelings that need to be acknowledged.

Monitor Symptoms

- Recognize Warning Signs: Learn to recognize the early signs of manic or depressive episodes. This can help in seeking timely intervention.
- Track Mood Changes: Keeping a mood diary can help track patterns and triggers, which can be useful for treatment adjustments.

Create a Supportive Environment

- Stable Routine: Encourage a regular routine for sleep, meals, and activities. Stability can help manage mood swings.
- <u>Healthy Lifestyle: Promote a healthy lifestyle, including regular exercise, a balanced diet, and avoiding alcohol and drugs</u>[2].
- Reduce Stress: Help minimize stress by creating a calm and supportive home environment.

Plan for Emergencies

- Crisis Plan: Work with your loved one to develop a crisis plan that outlines what to do if symptoms worsen. This plan should include emergency contacts, treatment preferences, and steps to take during a crisis.

* Emergency Contacts: Keep a list of healthcare providers and emergency contacts readily available.

Encourage Social Connections

* Stay Connected: Encourage your loved one to maintain social connections and engage in activities they enjoy. Social support is crucial for mental health.
* Join Support Groups: Support groups for individuals with bipolar disorder and their families can provide valuable insights and emotional support.

Take Care of Yourself

* Self-Care: Supporting someone with bipolar disorder can be demanding. Ensure you take time for self-care and seek support when needed.
* Set Boundaries: Establish healthy boundaries to prevent burnout and maintain your well-being.
* Seek Support: Consider joining a support group for caregivers or seeing a therapist to discuss your own feelings and challenges.

Legal Issues

Individuals with bipolar disorder may face various legal issues due to the nature of their condition, which can affect their behavior, decision-making, and interactions with the legal system.

Criminal Behavior and Legal Consequences

- Manic Episodes: During manic episodes, individuals may engage in impulsive and risky behaviors, such as reckless driving, theft, or substance abuse, which can lead to legal trouble.
- Impaired Judgment: The impaired judgment and lack of insight during manic or depressive episodes can result in actions that violate the law.
- Legal Defense: In some cases, individuals may use their mental health condition as part of their legal defense, arguing that their actions were a result of their disorder.

Involuntary Commitment

- Criteria for Commitment: Involuntary commitment may occur if an individual with bipolar disorder poses a danger to themselves or others, or is unable to care for themselves due to their condition.

- Legal Process: The process typically involves a legal hearing where evidence is presented to determine if involuntary hospitalization is necessary.
- Rights of the Individual: Individuals have the right to legal representation and to contest the commitment.

Employment and Discrimination

- Workplace Rights: Individuals with bipolar disorder are protected under the Americans with Disabilities Act (ADA), which prohibits discrimination based on disability.
- Reasonable Accommodations: Employers are required to provide reasonable accommodations to help individuals perform their job duties, such as flexible work hours or modified tasks.
- Disclosure: Deciding whether to disclose a bipolar disorder diagnosis to an employer is a personal choice. Disclosure can lead to accommodations but may also result in stigma or discrimination.

Guardianship and Conservatorship

- Legal Guardianship: In severe cases, a legal guardian may be appointed to make decisions on behalf of an individual with bipolar disorder who is unable to manage their affairs.

- Conservatorship: Similar to guardianship, conservatorship involves appointing a person to manage the financial affairs of someone who is unable to do so themselves.
- Rights and Responsibilities: Guardians and conservators have a legal duty to act in the best interest of the individual, and their actions are subject to court oversight.

Ethical Considerations in Treatment

- Informed Consent: Patients have the right to be informed about their treatment options, including the benefits and risks, and to make decisions about their care.
- Confidentiality: Healthcare providers must maintain the confidentiality of patient information, except in cases where there is a risk of harm to the patient or others.
- Involuntary Treatment: Ethical dilemmas arise when considering involuntary treatment for individuals who refuse care but are at risk of harm due to their condition.

Financial and Legal Planning

- Advance Directives: Individuals with bipolar disorder can create advance directives to outline their preferences for treatment and appoint a healthcare proxy to make decisions if they are unable to do so.
- Power of Attorney: Granting power of attorney allows a trusted person to make financial and legal decisions on behalf of the individual.
- Estate Planning: Proper estate planning can ensure that the individual's assets are managed according to their wishes and provide for their care.

Chapter 7

Conclusion

Bipolar disorder is a complex and multifaceted condition that affects millions of people worldwide. Throughout this book, we have explored the various aspects of bipolar disorder, from its symptoms and diagnosis to treatment options and coping strategies. As we conclude, it is essential to reflect on the key takeaways and the path forward for those living with this condition and their loved ones.

Understanding and Acceptance
One of the most critical steps in managing bipolar disorder is understanding and acceptance. Recognizing the signs and symptoms early can lead to timely intervention and better outcomes. Acceptance, both by the individual and their support network, is crucial in reducing stigma and fostering a supportive environment.

Treatment and Management

Effective management of bipolar disorder often requires a combination of medication, therapy, and lifestyle changes. Medications such as mood stabilizers, antipsychotics, and antidepressants can help manage symptoms, while therapy provides tools for coping with the emotional and psychological challenges. Additionally, lifestyle modifications, including regular exercise, a balanced diet, and adequate sleep, play a significant role in maintaining stability.

The Role of Support Systems

Support systems, including family, friends, and healthcare professionals, are vital in the journey of managing bipolar disorder. Open communication, empathy, and understanding from loved ones can make a significant difference in the individual's ability to cope with the condition. Support groups and community resources also offer valuable assistance and a sense of belonging.

Hope and Resilience

Living with bipolar disorder can be challenging, but it is important to remember that many people lead fulfilling and productive lives despite the condition. Building resilience through self-care, mindfulness, and stress management techniques can empower individuals to navigate the ups and downs of bipolar disorder. Hope is a powerful ally, and with the right support and treatment, it is possible to achieve stability and well-being.

Future Directions

Research in the field of bipolar disorder continues to advance, offering new insights and potential treatments. Ongoing studies aim to better understand the genetic, biological, and environmental factors contributing to the condition. As science progresses, there is hope for more effective and personalized treatment options that can improve the quality of life for those affected.

Final Thoughts

Bipolar disorder is a journey that requires patience, perseverance, and compassion. By fostering a deeper understanding, embracing effective treatment strategies, and building strong support networks, individuals with bipolar disorder can lead meaningful and fulfilling lives. Remember, you are not alone in this journey, and there is always hope for a brighter future.

Thank you for joining us on this exploration of bipolar disorder. May this book serve as a source of knowledge, comfort, and inspiration for all who read it.

Resources

Support Organizations

Here are some prominent support and advocacy organizations for bipolar disorder:

1. **Depression and Bipolar Support Alliance (DBSA)**: DBSA offers in-person and online support groups, educational resources, and advocacy for individuals living with depression and bipolar disorder.
2. **National Alliance on Mental Illness (NAMI)**: NAMI provides support, education, and advocacy for individuals with mental illnesses, including bipolar disorder. They offer various programs and resources to help individuals and their families.
3. **Mental Health America (MHA)**: MHA focuses on promoting mental health and preventing mental illness through advocacy, education, and support services.
4. **International Bipolar Foundation (IBPF)**: IBPF provides education, support, and resources for

individuals affected by bipolar disorder. They also engage in advocacy efforts to improve mental health care.

5. **American Psychiatric Association (APA)**: APA offers resources and support for mental health professionals and individuals affected by mental health conditions, including bipolar disorder.

6. **Mayo Clinic**: Mayo Clinic provides comprehensive information on bipolar disorder, including treatment options and support resources.

7. **National Institute of Mental Health (NIMH)**: NIMH conducts research and provides information on mental health conditions, including bipolar disorder. They offer resources for individuals, families, and healthcare providers.

Additional Reading

Here are some insightful reads to deepen your understanding of bipolar disorder:

1. **"Understanding Bipolar Disorder" by Mayo Clinic Press**: This article provides a comprehensive overview of bipolar disorder, including its symptoms, types, and treatment options.

2. **"Bipolar Disorder: Symptoms and Causes" by Mayo Clinic**: This resource delves into the symptoms, causes, and treatment of bipolar disorder, offering valuable insights into managing the condition.

3. **"Bipolar Disorder: Resources on Symptoms, Treatment, and More" by Medical News Today**: This collection of science-backed resources covers various aspects of bipolar disorder, including types, signs, risk factors, and management strategies.

4. **"Bipolar Disorder" by the National Institute of Mental Health (NIMH)**: This brochure presents detailed information on bipolar disorder, including symptoms, causes, diagnosis, treatment options, and resources for support.

5. **"Bipolar Disorder" by Mind**: This guide explains what bipolar disorder is, the available treatments, and self-help strategies. It also provides advice for friends and family on how to offer support.